The
Wiersbe
BIBLE STUDY SERIES

D1311604

The **Wiersbe**
BIBLE STUDY SERIES

PHILIPPIANS

Even When
Things Go
Wrong,
You Can
Have Joy

David C Cook®
transforming lives together

THE WIERSBE BIBLE STUDY SERIES: PHILIPPIANS
Published by David C Cook
4050 Lee Vance View
Colorado Springs, CO 80918 U.S.A.

David C Cook Distribution Canada
55 Woodslee Avenue, Paris, Ontario, Canada N3L 3E5

David C Cook U.K., Kingsway Communications
Eastbourne, East Sussex BN23 6NT, England

The graphic circle C logo is a registered trademark of David C Cook.

All rights reserved. Except for brief excerpts for review purposes,
no part of this book may be reproduced or used in any form
without written permission from the publisher.

All Scripture quotations in this study are taken from the *Holy Bible, New
International Version of the Bible*®. *NIV*®. Copyright © 1973, 1978, 1984
International Bible Society. Used by permission of Zondervan. All rights reserved.

In the *Be Joyful* excerpts, all Scripture quotations, unless otherwise noted, are taken from
the King James Version of the Bible. (Public Domain.) Scripture quotations marked PH
are taken from J. B. Phillips: *The New Testament in Modern English*, revised editions
© J. B. Phillips, 1958, 1960, 1972, permission of Macmillan Publishing Co. and Collins
Publishers; and NASB are taken from the *New American Standard Bible*,
© Copyright 1960, 1995 by The Lockman Foundation. Used by permission.
All excerpts taken from *Be Joyful*, second edition, published by David C Cook in 2008
© Warren W. Wiersbe, ISBN 978-1-4347-6846-9

ISBN 978-0-7814-4570-2
eISBN 978-1-4347-6565-9

© 2007 Warren W. Wiersbe

The Team: Steve Parolini, Gudmund Lee, Jack Campbell,
Theresa With, and Susan Vannaman
Series Cover Design: John Hamilton Design
Cover Photo: iStockphoto

Printed in the United States of America
First Edition 2007

8 9 10 11 12

040814

Contents

Introduction to Philippians

Jesus Christ was "a Man of sorrows and acquainted with grief" (Isa. 53:3 KJV). Yet, He possessed a deep joy that was beyond anything the world could offer.

Those who have trusted Christ have the privilege of experiencing "fullness of joy" (Ps. 16:11 KJV). However, few Christians take advantage of this privilege. They live under a cloud of disappointment when they could be walking in the sunshine of joy.

Thieves of Joy

Most of us must confess that when things are "going our way" we feel a lot happier and we are much easier to live with. But have you ever stopped to consider how few circumstances we actually control? We have no control over the weather or over the traffic or over the things other people say and do. The person whose happiness depends on ideal circumstances is going to be miserable much of the time. And yet here is the apostle Paul in the worst of circumstances, writing a letter saturated with joy!

All of us have lost joy because of people—what they are, what they say, and what they do. But we have to live and work with people; we cannot isolate ourselves and still live to glorify Christ.

And things! What thieves they can be. In the Sermon on the Mount, Jesus warned against storing up treasures on earth—they are not safe, they do not last, and they never satisfy. Yet most people today think that joy comes from the things they own.

Worry may be the worst thief of all. How many people have been robbed of peace and fulfillment because of anxiety? Worry even has physical consequences, and, while medicine can remove the symptoms, it cannot remove the cause. If Paul had wanted to worry, he had plenty of occasions. He was a political prisoner facing possible execution. His friends in Rome were divided in their attitudes toward his case. But in spite of these difficulties, Paul does not worry.

These, then, are the four thieves that rob us of joy: circumstances, people, things, and worry. How do we capture these thieves and keep them from taking away the joy that is rightfully ours in Christ? We must cultivate the right kind of mind.

Attitudes That Cultivate Joy

The reason many Christians are upset by circumstances is because they do not cultivate the "single mind." When a Christian is single-minded, he is concerned about the fellowship of the gospel, the furtherance of the gospel, and the faith of the gospel. Paul rejoiced in his circumstances because they helped strengthen his fellowship with other Christians, gave him opportunity to lead others to Christ, and enabled him to defend the gospel before the courts of Rome. When you have the single mind, your circumstances work for you, not against you.

In chapter 1 Paul puts Christ first, and in chapter 2 he puts others second, which means he puts himself last. If we go through life putting ourselves first, and others go through life doing the same thing, terrific battles will ensue. The Christian with the submissive mind *serves* others. He considers the good of others to be more important than his own plans and desires. In doing this, he discovers joy.

Most people mind earthly things, but the spiritually minded Christian looks at the things of this world from heaven's point of view. Like Paul, we must act and think as accountants with the right values, athletes with the right vigor, and aliens with the right vision. "I count … I press … I look" are the verbs that describe the man with a spiritual mind.

Finally, Paul describes the "secure mind" as one that counts on the spiritual resources of God's peace, God's power, and God's provision. With resources like these, there is no need to worry. Instead, we *overcome* worry when we practice right praying, right thinking, and right living.

What We Should Do

Paul's letter to the Philippians tells us that it is possible to live a life of Christian joy in spite of circumstances, people, and things, and that we don't need to worry when the going gets tough. How can we put this into practice?

First, be sure you are a Christian. You can't have the single mind, the submissive mind, the spiritual mind, or the secure mind unless you belong to Jesus Christ.

Second, admit your failures. The sooner we confess our sins to God, the sooner His joy will fill our lives.

Third, surrender your mind to Christ daily. When you find yourself losing your joy during the day, take inventory. If you are having a double mind or are dealing with pride or worry, confess your sin right then and there and ask God to restore your mind.

Finally, look for opportunities to put your mind to work. Learning and living go together, and God will give you the grace you need for every demand. As you practice exercising the right kind of attitude, you will find deep joy welling up in your heart.

Be joyful!

—*Warren W. Wiersbe*

How to Use This Study

This study is designed for both individual and small-group use. We've divided it into eight lessons—each references one or more chapters in Warren W. Wiersbe's commentary *Be Joyful*. While reading *Be Joyful* is not a prerequisite for going through this study, the additional insights and background Wiersbe offers can greatly enhance your study experience.

The **Getting Started** questions at the beginning of each lesson offer you an opportunity to record your first thoughts and reactions to the study text. This is an important step in the study process, as those "first impressions" often include clues about what it is your heart is longing to discover.

The bulk of the study is found in the **Going Deeper** questions. These dive into the Bible text and, along with helpful excerpts from Wiersbe's commentary, help you examine not only the original context and meaning of the verses but also modern application.

Looking Inward narrows the focus down to your personal story. These intimate questions can be a bit uncomfortable at times, but don't shy away from honesty here. This is where you are asked to stand before the mirror of God's Word and look closely at what you see. It's the place to take a good look at yourself in light of the lesson and search for ways in which you can grow in faith.

Going Forward is the place where you can commit to paper those things you want or need to do in order to better live out the discoveries you made in the "Looking Inward" section. Don't skip or skim through this. Take the time to really consider what practical steps you might take to move closer to Christ. Then share your thoughts with a trusted friend who can act as an encourager and accountability partner.

Finally, there is a brief **Seeking Help** section to close the lesson. This is a reminder for you to invite God into your spiritual-growth process. If you choose to write out a prayer in this section, come back to it as you work through the lesson and continue to seek the Holy Spirit's guidance as you discover God's will for your life.

Tips for Small Groups

A small group is a dynamic thing. One week it might seem like a group of close-knit friends. The next it might seem more like a group of uncomfortable strangers. A small-group leader's role is to read these subtle changes and adjust the tone of the discussion accordingly.

Small groups need to be safe places for people to talk openly. It is through shared wrestling with difficult life issues that some of the greatest personal growth is discovered. But in order for the group to feel safe, participants need to know it's okay *not* to share sometimes. Always invite honest disclosure, but never force someone to speak if he or she isn't comfortable doing so. (A savvy leader will follow up later with a group member who isn't comfortable sharing in a group setting to see if a one-on-one discussion is more appropriate.)

Have volunteers take turns reading excerpts from Scripture or from the commentary. The more each person is involved even in the mundane tasks, the more they'll feel comfortable opening up in more meaningful ways.

Finally, soak your group meetings in prayer—before you begin, during as needed, and always at the end of your time together.

Joy in Chains
(PHILIPPIANS 1:1–26)

Before you begin ...
- *Pray for the Holy Spirit to reveal truth and wisdom as you go through this lesson.*
- *Read Philippians 1:1–26. This lesson references chapters 2 and 3 in* Be Joyful. *It will be helpful for you to have your Bible and a copy of the commentary available as you work through this lesson.*

Getting Started

From the Commentary

In spite of his difficult circumstances as a prisoner in Rome, Paul was rejoicing. The secret of his joy was the *single mind;* he lived for Christ and the gospel. (Christ is named eighteen times in Philippians 1, and the gospel is mentioned six times.) "For to me to live is Christ, and to die is gain" (Phil. 1:21). But what really is "the single mind"? It is the attitude that says, "It makes no difference what happens to me, just as long as Christ is glorified and the gospel shared with others." Paul rejoiced in spite of his circumstances, because his circumstances strengthened the *fellowship of the gospel* (Phil. 1:1–11), promoted *the furtherance of the gospel* (Phil. 1:12–26), and guarded *the faith of the gospel* (Phil. 1:27–30).

—*Be Joyful*, page 29

1. What is your immediate reaction to this idea of rejoicing in spite of circumstances? How would you define joy?

More to Consider: Perhaps you know of someone who is experiencing particularly difficult circumstances. How might that person respond to Paul's rejoicing? Should faith in Christ automatically make it easier to rejoice in trials? Why or why not?

2. Choose one verse or phrase from Philippians 1:1–26 that stands out to you. This could be something you're intrigued by, something that makes you uncomfortable, something that puzzles you, something that resonates with you, or just something you want to examine further. Write that here. What strikes you about this verse? V, 24

Going Deeper

From the Commentary

> Isn't it remarkable that Paul was thinking of others and not of himself? As he awaited his trial in Rome, Paul's mind went back to the believers in Philippi, and every recollection he had brought him joy. Read Acts 16; you may discover that some things happened to Paul at Philippi, the memory of which could produce sorrow. He was illegally arrested and beaten, was placed in the stocks, and was humiliated before the people. But even those memories brought joy to Paul, because it was through this suffering that the jailer found Christ!
>
> —*Be Joyful*, pages 30–31

3. Underline all the times Paul references thankfulness or joy in Philippians 1:1–26. Trials tend to turn people inward—make them think of themselves and their own circumstances. What evidence does Paul offer in this passage for why he is able to think of others instead of himself?

4. Reread Philippians 1:7–8. Why do you think Paul says "It is right for me to feel this way about [the Philippian Christians]"? Why would anyone

think it wouldn't be right? What response do you think the Philippian Christians might have had to Paul's longing for them?

More to Consider: If your church sponsors or supports missionaries, take a few moments to pray for them. Consider paraphrasing Paul's prayer in Philippians 1:9–11.

From the Commentary

What is the "fruit" God wants to see from our lives? Certainly He wants the "fruit of the Spirit" (Gal. 5:22–23), Christian character that glorifies God. Paul compared winning lost souls to Christ to bearing fruit (Rom. 1:13), and he also names "holiness" as a spiritual fruit (Rom. 6:22). He exhorted us to be "fruitful in every good work" (Col. 1:10), and the writer to the Hebrews reminded us that our praise is the "fruit of our lips" (Heb. 13:15).

The fruit tree does not make a great deal of noise when it produces its crop; it merely allows the life within to work

in a natural way, and fruit is the result. "He that abideth
in me, and I in him, the same bringeth forth much fruit:
for without me ye can do nothing" (John 15:5).

—*Be Joyful*, page 35

5. Paul's prayer encourages the Philippians to be filled with the "fruit of
righteousness." What is this fruit? How does being fruitful bring joy?

From Today's World

In March 2007, a bus carrying a small college's baseball team plunged over
an overpass, killing four students and the husband-and-wife drivers. The
accident was likely the result of an error of judgment by the driver, who
mistook an exit ramp for a lane and sped off over the guardrail.

Stories like this are always tragic, not only for the families of those
whose loved ones are killed, but for those who survived as well.

6. Read Philippians 1:12. Paul is referring to his imprisonment in this
verse. In what ways might his difficult circumstances serve to advance the
gospel? How can tragedies like the accident described above also advance
the gospel? What other circumstances or "chains" might be used to advance
the gospel?

From the Commentary

> More than anything else, Paul's desire as a missionary
> was to preach the gospel in Rome. The hub of the great
> empire, Rome was the key city of its day. If Paul could
> conquer it for Christ, it would mean reaching millions
> with the message of salvation. It was critically important
> on Paul's agenda, for he said, "After I have been there
> [Jerusalem], I must also see Rome" (Acts 19:21). From
> Corinth he wrote, "So, as much as in me is, I am ready
> [eager] to preach the gospel to you that are at Rome also"
> (Rom. 1:15).
>
> —*Be Joyful*, page 39

7. Paul's plan to preach in Rome was interrupted by his imprisonment.
How did this impact his goal? In what ways did God still reach the people
of Rome? How did God use Paul's chains to advance the gospel?

More to Consider: Paul's story is one of turning failure into success.
What are some other success-story examples from the Bible or from

your own life experience? What do these stories tell you about how to stay positive in light of difficult circumstances?

From the Commentary

God still wants His children to take the gospel into new areas. He wants us to be pioneers, and sometimes He arranges circumstances so that we can be nothing else but pioneers. In fact, that is how the gospel originally came to Philippi. Paul had tried to enter other territory, but God had repeatedly shut the door (Acts 16:6–10). Paul wanted to take the message eastward into Asia, but God directed him to take it westward into Europe. What a difference it would have made in the history of mankind if Paul had been permitted to follow his own plan.

—*Be Joyful,* pages 40–41

8. What might Paul have felt when the Holy Spirit first changed his plans to enter Asia? When he was arrested and placed in chains? How might Paul's impact on the Roman guards have been different had he been disappointed or upset with God?

9. Reread Philippians 1:15–18. What does it look like to preach out of envy and rivalry? Paul makes a powerful claim that it doesn't matter how Christ is preached … just that He is. What is your reaction to this? In what sorts of different ways have you heard Christ preached?

From the Commentary

Paul was not afraid of life or death. Either way, he wanted to magnify Christ in his body. No wonder he had joy!

—*Be Joyful,* page 46

10. Philippians 1:21 is an oft-quoted verse, but the verses that follow shed important light on Paul's unselfish statement. Circle all of Paul's "pros" for living and underline the "cons." How can overcoming a fear of death bring joy?

Looking Inward

Take a moment to reflect on all that you've explored thus far in this study of Philippians 1:1–26. Review your notes and answers and think about how each of these things matters in your life today.

Tips for Small Groups: To get the most out of this section, form pairs or trios and have group members take turns answering these questions. Be honest and as open as you can in this discussion, but most of all, be encouraging and supportive of others. Be sensitive to those who are going through particularly difficult times and don't press for people to speak if they're uncomfortable doing so.

11. In what ways are you, like Paul, defending or confirming the gospel? What challenges or trials are you facing as you do this? If you're not sharing the gospel, what is holding you back from doing so?

12. Paul rejoices even in the midst of many trials. Is this easy for you to do? Why or why not? What makes it a challenge to remain joyful when the plans you had go awry? What in Paul's letter can help you discover that joy?

13. As you read Paul's examination of which is better—to live and preach the gospel of Christ, or to die and be with Christ—which side of that argument compels you most? Why? How can you find joy in either circumstance? What fruitful labor can you pursue if you "remain in the body"?

Going Forward

14. Think of one or two things that you have learned that you'd like to work on in the coming week. Remember that this is all about quality, not quantity. It's better to work on one specific area of life and do it well than to work on many and do poorly (or to be so overwhelmed that you simply don't try).

Do you need to discover patience in trials? Learn how to be joyful in difficult circumstances? Trust God's plans when they don't match your own? What does working on this look like in practical terms? Be specific. Go back through Philippians 1:1–26 and put a star next to the phrase or verse that is most encouraging to you. Consider memorizing this verse so it can encourage you when you most need it.

Real-Life Application Ideas: Find a book on Christian martyrs, such as Jesus Freaks *or* Foxe's Book of Martyrs, *and study the lives of these people of faith. Examine how their lives line up with what Paul is teaching in Philippians 1:1–26.*

Seeking Help

15. Write a prayer below (or simply pray one in silence), inviting God to work on your mind and heart in the areas you noted above. Be honest about your desires and fears.

Notes for Small Groups:

- *Look for ways to put into practice the things you wrote in the Going Forward section in this lesson. Talk with other group members about your ideas and commit to being accountable to one another.*

- *During the coming week, ask the Holy Spirit to continue to reveal truth to you from what you've read and studied.*

- *Before you start the next lesson, read Philippians 1:27–30. For more in-depth lesson preparation, read chapter 4, "Battle Stations!" in* Be Joyful.

The Battlefield
(PHILIPPIANS 1:27–30)

Before you begin ...
- *Pray for the Holy Spirit to reveal truth and wisdom as you go through this lesson.*
- *Read Philippians 1:27–30. This lesson references chapter 4 in* Be Joyful. *It will be helpful for you to have your Bible and a copy of the commentary available as you work through this lesson.*

Getting Started

From the Commentary

> The Christian life is not a playground; it is a battle-ground. We are *sons* in the family, enjoying the *fellowship* of the gospel (Phil. 1:1–11); we are *servants* sharing in the *furtherance* of the gospel (Phil. 1:12–26); but we are also *soldiers* defending the *faith* of the gospel.
>
> —*Be Joyful,* page 51

1. What is your immediate reaction to Wiersbe's claim that the Christian life is a battleground? In what ways do you see truth in this statement?

More to Consider: In Be Joyful, *Wiersbe goes on to say, "the believer with the single mind can have the joy of the Holy Spirit even in the midst of battle." What makes a single-minded believer special? How does the "joy of the Holy Spirit" compare to what we might call happiness?*

2. Choose one verse or phrase from Philippians 1:27–30 that stands out to you. This could be something you're intrigued by, something that makes you uncomfortable, something that puzzles you, something that resonates with you, or just something you want to examine further. Write that here. What strikes you about this verse?

Going Deeper

From the Commentary

> If Satan can only rob believers of their Christian faith, the doctrines that are distinctively theirs, then he can cripple and defeat the ministry of the gospel. It is sad to hear people say, "I don't care what you believe, just so long as you live right." What we believe determines how we behave, and wrong belief ultimately means a wrong life.
>
> —*Be Joyful,* pages 51–52

3. Describe an example or two of how a person's beliefs determine their actions. In what way is Paul underlining this truth when he writes, "Whatever happens, conduct yourselves in a manner worthy of the gospel of Christ" in Philippians 1:27?

From the Commentary

> How can a group of Christians fight this enemy? "For the weapons of our warfare are not of the flesh" (2 Cor.

10:4 nasb). Peter took up a sword in the garden, and Jesus rebuked him (John 18:10–11). We use spiritual weapons—the Word of God and prayer (Eph. 6:11–18; Heb. 4:12), and we must depend on the Holy Spirit to give us the power that we need.

—Be Joyful, page 52

4. Paul longs for the Philippian Christians to "stand firm in one spirit." What does he mean by this? What is the outward evidence of someone who depends on the Holy Spirit for his or her power?

More to Consider: Read Hebrews 4:12 and Ephesians 6:11–18. Circle the spiritual weapons described in these passages. How have you seen each of these used in "battles"?

From the Commentary

The most important weapon against the enemy is not a stirring sermon or a powerful book; it is the consistent life of believers.

—Be Joyful, page 52

5. Paul encourages readers to be consistent in their behavior and actions, according to their faith. Why is a consistent "life of faith" such a powerful witness to nonbelievers? What does this suggest about the way we, as Christians, can most effectively reach others with the gospel?

From the Commentary

> Paul was suggesting that we Christians are the citizens of heaven, and while we are on earth we ought to behave like heaven's citizens. He brought this concept up again in Philippians 3:20. It would be a very meaningful expression to the people in Philippi because Philippi was a Roman colony, and its citizens were actually Roman citizens, protected by Roman law. The church of Jesus Christ is a colony of heaven on earth. And we ought to behave like the citizens of heaven.
>
> —*Be Joyful,* page 53

6. Skim back over Philippians 1. Circle any phrase that describes someone who is a citizen of heaven. What other traits might describe a citizen of heaven?

From Today's World

A quick scan of your phone book's yellow pages will illustrate rather vividly how many different churches there are in a given city. What differentiates these churches? Theology, certainly. Worship style. Culture. All of these play a factor. But how did we get to this segmented place? Church splits have played a large role in the creation of so many different denominations, so many different churches. One church even split because of a disagreement on the placement of a piano bench. This led to two different factions taking turns in the church, moving the bench in and out according to who was occupying the building at the time!

7. What are some common issues that tend to divide church members? When a church is arguing amongst itself, what message does this send to nonbelievers? How can a church that is struggling in this area turn things around and become more consistent in its behavior?

From the Commentary

> Paul pictured the church as a team, and he reminded them that it is teamwork that wins victories....
>
> Keep in mind that there was division in the church at Philippi. For one thing, two women were not getting along with each other (Phil. 4:2). Apparently the members of the fellowship were taking sides, as is often the case, and the resulting division was hindering the work of the church.
>
> —*Be Joyful,* page 54

8. What sort of team is your church or small group? What are its strengths? Weaknesses? In what ways has division hindered the work of your church or small group?

More to Consider: Study the difference between a successful team and an unsuccessful one (teams you're familiar with either in the workplace or on the ball field). What are the common characteristics of a successful team? An unsuccessful one? What insights can you gain from this that apply to your church or small group? To your family?

From the Commentary

> The presence of conflict is *a privilege;* we suffer "for his sake." In fact, Paul told us that this conflict is "granted" to us—it is a gift! If we were suffering for ourselves, it would be no privilege, but because we are suffering for and with Christ, it is a high and holy honor. After all, He suffered for us, and a willingness to suffer for Him is the very least we can do to show our love and gratitude.
>
> —*Be Joyful,* page 56

9. Read Philippians 1:29. What sort of conflict has your church or small group experienced? Are all struggles "gifts"? Why or why not? In what ways might you see any of your current struggles as "gifts"? (Keep in mind Paul is writing this from prison and in the middle of many struggles himself.)

From the Commentary

> Actually, going through spiritual conflict is one way we have *to grow in Christ.* God gives us the strength we need to stand firm against the enemy, and this confidence is proof to him that he will lose and we are on the winning side (Phil. 1:28).
>
> —*Be Joyful,* page 57

10. Take a moment to consider the spiritual growth you've seen in your church (in leadership, members, family, and friends). What circumstances brought about that growth? What makes the difference between a group that splinters because of struggle and one that grows?

Looking Inward

Take a moment to reflect on all that you've explored thus far in this study of Philippians 1:27–30. Review your notes and answers and think about how each of these things matters in your life today.

Tips for Small Groups: To get the most out of this section, form pairs or trios and have group members take turns answering these questions.

Be honest and as open as you can in this discussion, but most of all, be encouraging and supportive of others. Be sensitive to those who are going through particularly difficult times and don't press for people to speak if they're uncomfortable doing so.

11. In what ways have you maintained a consistent witness for Christ? What specific behaviors or attitudes post a challenge to that consistency?

12. Think about a time when you may have been the cause or catalyst for division in a group or team. What prompted that behavior or action? What was the result? If the result was negative, what might you have done differently to turn that around?

13. How do you feel when you consider what Paul states—that suffering is "granted" to Christians (that it is a gift)? Is it easy for you to see suffering as a gift? Why or why not?

Going Forward

14. Think of one or two things that you have learned that you'd like to work on in the coming week. Remember that this is all about quality, not quantity. It's better to work on one specific area of life and do it well than to work on many and do poorly (or to be so overwhelmed that you simply don't try).

Do you need to work on the consistency of your witness? What areas of your life need the most work? Do you need to change your perspective on current suffering? How will you do that? What does working on this look like in practical terms? Be specific. Go back through Philippians 1:27–30 and put a star next to the phrase or verse that speaks to your greatest area of challenge. Consider memorizing this verse so it can help you be consistent in your faith.

Real-Life Application Ideas: Meet with your closest friend over coffee or lunch and talk specifically about how well you're living a consistent witness for Christ. Invite that friend's wisdom into your life and talk together about practical ways to move toward a more consistent behavior. Be humble and willing to listen during this time and be sure to spend some of the time in prayer together.

Seeking Help

15. Write a prayer below (or simply pray one in silence), inviting God to work on your mind and heart in the areas you noted above. Be honest about your desires and fears.

Notes for Small Groups:

- *Look for ways to put into practice the things you wrote in the Going Forward section in this lesson. Talk with other group members about your ideas and commit to being accountable to one another.*
- *During the coming week, ask the Holy Spirit to continue to reveal truth to you from what you've read and studied.*
- *Before you start the next lesson, read Philippians 2:1–11. For more in-depth lesson preparation, read chapter 5, "The Great Example," in* Be Joyful.

Like Minded
(PHILIPPIANS 2:1–11)

Before you begin ...
- *Pray for the Holy Spirit to reveal truth and wisdom as you go through this lesson.*
- *Read Philippians 2:1–11. This lesson references chapter 5 in* Be Joyful. *It will be helpful for you to have your Bible and a copy of the commentary available as you work through this lesson.*

Getting Started

From the Commentary

People can rob us of our joy. Paul was facing his problems with people at Rome (Phil. 1:15–18) as well as with people in Philippi, and it was the latter who concerned him the most. When Epaphroditus brought a generous gift from the church in Philippi, and good news of the church's concern for Paul, he also brought the bad news of a possible division in the church family....

Paul knew what some church workers today do not know: There is a difference between *unity* and *uniformity*. True spiritual unity comes from within; it is a matter of the heart. Uniformity is the result of pressure from without.

—*Be Joyful,* page 61

1. What is your initial reaction to the definitions of *unity* and *uniformity*? Which word best describes your church? Explain your answer.

More to Consider: Philippians 2:1–11 focuses on the idea of imitating Christ's humility. When you look at your church or small group, what are some great examples of humility in action? (And remember, true humility doesn't seek attention—it's all about other-mindedness.)

2. Choose one verse or phrase from Philippians 2:1–11 that stands out to you. This could be something you're intrigued by, something that makes you uncomfortable, something that puzzles you, something that resonates

with you, or just something you want to examine further. Write that here. What strikes you about this verse?

Going Deeper

3. Reread Philippians 2:5–11. Underline "Your attitude should be ..." (or however your Bible's translation reads at the beginning of 2:5) and then circle phrases or words that follow to complete that statement. What does this tell you about what it means to be "like Christ"?

From the Commentary

> The secret of joy in spite of circumstances is *the single mind.* The secret of joy in spite of people is *the submissive mind.* The key verse is "Let nothing be done through

strife or vainglory; but in lowliness of mind let each esteem other better [more important] than themselves" (Phil. 2:3). In Philippians 1, it is "Christ first" and in Philippians 2 it is "others next." Paul the soul winner in Philippians 1 becomes Paul the servant in Philippians 2.

—*Be Joyful*, page 62

4. What images or thoughts come to mind when you read or hear that word *submissive*? What are the negative implications of that word? What definition does Paul offer for the submissive mind in 2:1–11?

More to Consider: Wiersbe goes on to say that "the 'submissive mind' does not mean that the believer is at the beck and call of everybody else or that he is a 'religious doormat' for everybody to use!" When have you observed this type of behavior in others? In yourself? What do you think drives this sort of behavior? How is that different from humility?

From the Commentary

> Jesus Christ did not need anything. He had all the glory
> and praise of heaven. With the Father and the Spirit,
> He reigned over the universe. But Philippians 2:6 states
> an amazing fact: He did not consider His equality with
> God as something selfishly to be held on to. Jesus did not
> think of Himself; He thought of others. His outlook (or
> attitude) was that of unselfish concern for others. This
> is "the mind of Christ," an attitude that says, "I cannot
> keep my privileges for myself, I must use them for oth-
> ers, and to do this, I will gladly lay them aside and pay
> whatever price is necessary."
>
> —*Be Joyful,* page 63

5. What does "unselfish concern for others" look like in practical terms?
What is the price you must pay to use your privileges for others?

From Today's World

Humility is not a trait that typically is referenced when talking about rock
stars or actors or public figures in general. Take a moment to recall the

headlines from today's paper (or online news sites). If you have a newspaper or computer handy, go there now to do your review. Look for stories or articles about famous people and skim the content of those stories.

6. Did you find examples of humility in the articles you reviewed? Why is boasting or self-aggrandizing so much a part of popular culture? If true humility is something that doesn't seek attention, how can people in the public eye be humble? What about well-known servants like Mother Teresa? How might the tenor of the news change if more stories reported on other-mindedness instead of selfish or narcissistic behavior?

From the Commentary

Thinking of "others" in an abstract sense only is insufficient; we must get down to the nitty-gritty of true service. A famous philosopher wrote glowing words about educating children but abandoned his own. It was easy for him to love children in the abstract, but when it came down to practice, that was something else. Jesus thought of others *and became a servant.*

—*Be Joyful,* page 65

7. What are some examples you've observed of people who've gotten down to the "nitty-gritty of true service"? What do you think was their motivation for this service?

More to Consider: If you're like most people, you probably feel overwhelmed when you hear about a global disaster or some catastrophic event that results in loss of life. In what ways is this an example of responding in the "abstract"? Are there ways to move from an abstract response to a nitty-gritty one? Think of a specific example of what the nitty-gritty might look like.

From the Commentary

Many people are willing to serve others *if* it does not cost them anything. But if there is a price to pay, they suddenly lose interest. Jesus "became obedient unto death, even the death of the cross" (Phil. 2:8). His was not the death of a martyr but the death of a Savior. He willingly laid down His life for the sins of the world.

—*Be Joyful*, pages 66–67

8. Do all acts of service include a cost? What are some examples of service where the cost is low? Where the cost is high? Is there a correlation between the cost and the benefit? Why or why not?

From the Commentary

> It is one of the paradoxes of the Christian life that the more we give, the more we receive; the more we sacrifice, the more God blesses. This is why the submissive mind leads to joy; it makes us more like Christ. This means sharing His joy as we also share in His sufferings.
>
> —*Be Joyful,* page 68

9. As you look at Philippians 2:1–11, what evidence do you find to support this paradox that "the more we give, the more we receive"? How does this compare to what popular culture says about giving? About blessing?

From the Commentary

> This, of course, is the great goal of all that we do—to glorify God. Paul warns us against "vainglory" in Philippians 2:3. The kind of rivalry that pits Christian against Christian and ministry against ministry is not spiritual, nor is it satisfying. It is vain, empty. Jesus humbled Himself for others, and God highly exalted Him; the result of this exaltation is glory to God.
>
> —*Be Joyful,* page 68

10. When have you seen or experienced this "vainglory" Wiersbe writes about? What does it feel like to know that in serving others, you are glorifying God?

Looking Inward

Take a moment to reflect on all that you've explored thus far in this study of Philippians 2:1–11. Review your notes and answers and think about how each of these things matters in your life today.

Tips for Small Groups: To get the most out of this section, form pairs or trios and have group members take turns answering these questions. Be honest and as open as you can in this discussion, but most of all, be encouraging and supportive of others. Be sensitive to those who are going through particularly difficult times and don't press for people to speak if they're uncomfortable doing so.

11. Would you describe yourself as someone who has a submissive mind when it comes to matters of faith? Why or why not? What personality traits or behaviors make it a challenge for you to submit yourself to Christ?

12. What are some of the nitty-gritty ways you serve others? What is your motivation for these acts of service?

13. What does true humility look like to you? How well are you living this out in your life?

Going Forward

14. Think of one or two things that you have learned that you'd like to work on in the coming week. Remember that this is all about quality, not quantity. It's better to work on one specific area of life and do it well than to work on many and do poorly (or to be so overwhelmed that you simply don't try).

Do you need to learn what it means to submit yourself to Christ? To be more humble? To find ways to serve in the nitty-gritty? Perhaps you are feeling a specific prompting to live out some truth you've discovered in the Bible. Write these thoughts below. Be specific. Go back through Philippians 2:1–11 and put a star next to the phrase or verse that speaks to something you desire to work on in your life. Consider memorizing this verse so it can challenge you and move you toward positive change.

Real-Life Application Ideas: Get involved in a nitty-gritty act of service. Talk with the leaders in your church or contact local service organizations to find out what your options are. Then, as you consider your options, choose one that doesn't feel comfortable, one that doesn't bring attention to you. Serve humbly.

Seeking Help

15. Write a prayer below (or simply pray one in silence), inviting God to work on your mind and heart in the areas you noted above. Be honest about your desires and fears.

Notes for Small Groups:

- *Look for ways to put into practice the things you wrote in the Going Forward section in this lesson. Talk with other group members about your ideas and commit to being accountable to one another.*

- *During the coming week, ask the Holy Spirit to continue to reveal truth to you from what you've read and studied.*

- *Before you start the next lesson, read Philippians 2:12–30. For more in-depth lesson preparation, read chapters 6 and 7, "The Ins and Outs of Christian Living" and "A Priceless Pair," in* Be Joyful.

Christian Living
(PHILIPPIANS 2:12–30)

Before you begin ...
- *Pray for the Holy Spirit to reveal truth and wisdom as you go through this lesson.*
- *Read Philippians 2:12–30. This lesson references chapters 6 and 7 in* Be Joyful. *It will be helpful for you to have your Bible and a copy of the commentary available as you work through this lesson.*

Getting Started

From the Commentary

The Christian life is not a series of ups and downs. It is rather a process of "ins and outs." God works *in,* and we work *out.* We cultivate the submissive mind by responding to the divine provisions God makes available to us.

—*Be Joyful,* page 74

1. In what ways do you see the Christian life as a series of ups and downs? How does Paul's encouragement for how to live the Christian life (Phil. 2:12–18) illustrate what Wiersbe states above: that it is more of a series of ins and outs?

2. Choose one verse or phrase from Philippians 2:12–30 that stands out to you. This could be something you're intrigued by, something that makes you uncomfortable, something that puzzles you, something that resonates with you, or just something you want to examine further. Write that here. What strikes you about this verse?

Going Deeper

From the Commentary

> "Work out your own salvation" (Phil. 2:12) does not suggest, "Work *for* your own salvation." To begin with, Paul

was writing to people who were already "saints" (Phil. 1:1), which means they had trusted Christ and had been set apart for Him. The verb "work out" carries the meaning of "work to full completion," such as working out a problem in mathematics. In Paul's day it was also used for "working a mine," that is, getting out of the mine all the valuable ore possible; or "working a field" so as to get the greatest harvest possible.

—*Be Joyful,* page 74

3. What comes to mind when you read that command, "Work out your salvation"? According to Paul, how is this accomplished?

From the Commentary

Paul did not admonish us to retreat from the world and go into a spiritual isolation ward. It is only as we are confronted with the needs and problems of real life that we can begin to become more like Christ. The Pharisees were so isolated and insulated from reality that they developed an artificial kind of self-righteousness that

was totally unlike the righteousness God wanted them
to have.

—*Be Joyful,* page 76

4. What are your greatest challenges to being Christlike in real life? What
is tempting about the "spiritual isolation" Wiersbe describes? How is Paul's
admonition in 2:12–16 similar to the idea of being in the world but not of it?

*More to Consider: Read John 14:16–17, 26; Acts 1:8; and 1
Corinthians 6:19–20. What do these verses tell us about the source of
power that allows us to be Christlike? How do we go about counting
on the Holy Spirit's power?*

From the Commentary

We must also *appropriate* the Word—"receive it." This
means much more than listening to it, or even reading and
studying it. To "receive" God's Word means to welcome it
and make it a part of our inner being. God's truth is to the
spiritual man what food is to the physical man.

—*Be Joyful,* page 77

5. What are some specific ways we can appropriate the Word? What is Paul inviting us to receive in Philippians 2:12–18?

From the Commentary

> The Word of God, prayer, and suffering are the three tools that God uses in our lives. Just as electricity must run through a conductor, so the Holy Spirit must work through the means God has provided.
>
> —*Be Joyful,* page 79

6. How does the Holy Spirit work through God's Word, prayer, and suffering? What other means does the Holy Spirit use to work in our lives? What actions on our part are required in order to allow the Spirit to work? (See 2:12, 14, 16.)

From the Commentary

> There is a twofold joy that comes to the person who possesses and practices the submissive mind: a joy hereafter (Phil. 2:16) and a joy here and now (Phil. 2:17–18). In the day of Christ (see Phil. 1:10), God is going to reward those who have been faithful to Him. "The joy of thy Lord" is going to be a part of that reward (Matt. 25:21). The faithful Christian will discover that his sufferings on earth have been transformed into glory in heaven. He will see that his work was not in vain (1 Cor. 15:58). It was this same kind of promise of future joy that helped our Savior in His sufferings on the cross (Heb. 12:1–2).
>
> —*Be Joyful*, page 80

7. What are other examples in life where the joy happens both now and later? Are there times when waiting for the day of Christ for your joy doesn't seem like enough? Why or why not? Where does Paul find his strength to rejoice even in sacrifice (v. 17)?

From the Commentary

> [Paul] knew that his readers would be prone to say, "It is impossible for us to follow such examples as Christ and Paul! After all, Jesus is the very Son of God, and Paul is a chosen apostle who has had great spiritual experiences!" For this reason, Paul introduced us to two ordinary saints, men who were not apostles or spectacular miracle workers. He wanted us to know that the submissive mind is not a luxury enjoyed by a chosen few; it is a necessity for Christian joy, and an opportunity for *all* believers.
>
> —*Be Joyful,* page 86

8. Based on what Paul writes, what makes Timothy and Epaphroditus "saints" as Wiersbe describes them? Name some other ordinary saints (from the Bible or history or even from your own life). What makes them both ordinary and saintlike?

More to Consider: Read Mark 1:14–20 and 3:13–19 where Jesus chooses His disciples. In what ways are Jesus' disciples examples of ordinary saints?

From the Commentary

> Paul did not add Timothy to his "team" the very day the
> boy was saved. Paul was too wise to make an error like
> that. He left him behind to become a part of the church
> fellowship in Derbe and Lystra, and it was in that fellow-
> ship that Timothy grew in spiritual matters and learned
> how to serve the Lord.
>
> —*Be Joyful*, page 87

9. Make a brief list of ways your church helps to prepare you and others for living the Christian life. What happens when someone who isn't spiritually mature attempts to lead or teach others? How does a spiritually mature Christian act and think? (Skim the rest of Philippians chapter 2 for some of Paul's answers to this question.)

From the Commentary

> Like Timothy, Epaphroditus was concerned about others.… Our churches today need men and women who are burdened for missions and for those in difficult places of Christian service. "The problem in our churches," states one missionary leader, "is that we have too many spectators and not enough participants." Epaphroditus was not content simply to contribute to the offering. He gave *himself to* help carry the offering!
>
> —*Be Joyful,* page 91

10. What are some examples of Christian service your church or small group offers? How does your church support missionaries? What sort of involvement does the rest of the church body have with that ministry? With local missions organizations? What do you see as the areas in need of most improvement when it comes to Christian service?

More to Consider: Paul encourages the Philippian church to honor Epaphroditus by welcoming him with great joy. First Thessalonians

5:12–13 tells us it's not wrong to honor those who serve. Who are some of the people in your church or community worthy of honoring for their service? What are some ways your church or small group honors those who serve?

Looking Inward

Take a moment to reflect on all that you've explored thus far in this study of Philippians 2:12–30. Review your notes and answers and think about how each of these things matters in your life today.

Tips for Small Groups: To get the most out of this section, form pairs or trios and have group members take turns answering these questions. Be honest and as open as you can in this discussion, but most of all, be encouraging and supportive of others. Be sensitive to those who are going through particularly difficult times and don't press for people to speak if they're uncomfortable doing so.

11. How are you "working out your salvation"? What practical steps are you taking toward that end? What challenges are you facing as you attempt to do this?

12. Review Philippians 2:14–16. Do you "do everything without complaining or arguing"? How can you improve in this area of your life? Who would benefit most from this improvement?

13. What about your Christian walk might prompt others to see you as an "ordinary saint"? How does this make you feel? How can you expand these areas in your life?

Going Forward

14. Think of one or two things that you have learned that you'd like to work on in the coming week. Remember that this is all about quality, not quantity. It's better to work on one specific area of life and do it well than to work on many and do poorly (or to be so overwhelmed that you simply don't try).

Do you desire to learn more about working out your salvation? Do you want to discover how to live a more sacrificial life? Are you interested in serving? Perhaps you are feeling a specific prompting to live out some truth you've discovered in the Bible. Write these thoughts below. Be specific. Go back through Philippians 2:12–30 and put a star next to the phrase or verse that is speaking most directly to your heart right now. Consider memorizing this verse as evidence that you have accepted it into your life.

Real-Life Application Ideas: Plan and run a celebration for the "ordinary saints" in your life. Share a meal and fellowship together and give each ordinary servant a thank-you card, delineating the reason you see him or her as a saint.

Seeking Help

15. Write a prayer below (or simply pray one in silence), inviting God to work on your mind and heart in the areas you noted above. Be honest about your desires and fears.

Notes for Small Groups:

- *Look for ways to put into practice the things you wrote in the Going Forward section in this lesson. Talk with other group members about your ideas and commit to being accountable to one another.*

- *During the coming week, ask the Holy Spirit to continue to reveal truth to you from what you've read and studied.*

- *Before you start the next lesson, read Philippians 3:1–11. For more in-depth lesson preparation, read chapter 8, "Learning How to Count," in* Be Joyful.

New Values
(PHILIPPIANS 3:1–11)

Before you begin ...
- *Pray for the Holy Spirit to reveal truth and wisdom as you go through this lesson.*
- *Read Philippians 3:1–11. This lesson references chapter 8 in* Be Joyful. *It will be helpful for you to have your Bible and a copy of the commentary available as you work through this lesson.*

Getting Started

From the Commentary

Circumstances and people can rob us of joy, but so can *things,* and it is this "thief" that Paul deals with in Philippians 3.... The key word in Philippians 3:1–11 is *count* (Phil. 3:7–8). In the Greek, two different words are used, but the basic idea is the same: to evaluate, to assess. "The unexamined life is not worth living," Socrates said. Yet few people sit down to weigh seriously the values that control their decisions and directions. Many people today are the slaves of "things," and as a result do not experience real Christian joy.

—Be Joyful, pages 95–96

1. How does someone go about examining his or her life? What are the key values that must be examined in this process?

More to Consider: Make a list of values that shape your decisions and directions. Keep this handy as you go through the rest of this study and compare what you've written to what you discover.

2. Choose one verse or phrase from Philippians 3:1–11 that stands out to you. This could be something you're intrigued by, something that makes you uncomfortable, something that puzzles you, something that resonates with you, or just something you want to examine further. Write that here. What strikes you about this verse?

Going Deeper

From the Commentary

> Like most religious people today, Paul had enough morality to keep him out of trouble, but not enough righteousness to get him into heaven. It was not bad things that kept Paul away from Jesus—it was good things. He had to lose his religion to find salvation.
>
> —*Be Joyful,* page 96

3. Have you met people who believe morality is enough to get them into heaven? They're in good company! Paul believed this for a time too. In what ways does Paul describe how to "lose your religion" in Philippians 3:1–11? How might you rewrite Paul's illustration for today's seeker?

From the Commentary

> From the very beginning, the gospel came "to the Jew first" (see Acts 3:26; Rom. 1:16), so that the first seven chapters of Acts deal only with Jewish believers or with Gentiles who were Jewish proselytes (Acts 2:10). In Acts

8:5–25, the message went to the Samaritans, but this did not cause too much of an upheaval since the Samaritans were at least partly Jewish. But when Peter went to the Gentiles in Acts 10, this created an uproar. Peter was called on the carpet to explain his activities (Acts 11). After all, the Gentiles in Acts 10 had become Christians *without first becoming Jews,* and this was a whole new thing for the church. Peter explained that it was God who had directed him to preach to the Gentiles, and the matter seemed to be settled.

—*Be Joyful,* page 97

4. How is the situation Paul is dealing with in Philippians 3:1–6 like that which the church still faces today? In what ways do Christians still have trouble accepting those who come to faith through unfamiliar circumstances? What other kinds of judgments are passed today within the Christian church?

From the Commentary

Here Paul used a pun on the word *circumcision.* The word translated "circumcision" literally means "a mutilation."

The Judaizers taught that circumcision was essential to salvation (Acts 15:1; Gal. 6:12–18), but Paul stated that circumcision of *itself* is only a mutilation. The true Christian has experienced a spiritual circumcision in Christ (Col. 2:11), and does not need any fleshly operations. Circumcision, baptism, the Lord's supper, tithing, or any other religious practice cannot save a person from his sins. Only faith in Jesus Christ can do that.

—*Be Joyful,* page 99

5. Take a close look at your church or small group. Do you see any implicit or explicit "requirements" that look like what Paul is speaking against in Philippians 3:1–6? Does your church or small group hold tight to any "circumcisions"? If so, list them here.

More to Consider: Read John 4:19–24. How does this passage relate to what Paul is writing about in Philippians 3:1–6?

From Today's World

In an interview, outspoken singer Elton John stated that "organized religion … turns people into really hateful lemmings and it's not really compassionate." He went on to question why religious leaders aren't coming together to do anything about the conflicts in the world. He asked, "Why aren't they having a conclave? Why aren't they coming together?"*

6. What is your response to Elton John's bold statements? Is there a sliver (or more) of truth in his claim? If so, what is it? What sorts of things keep Christians from being at the forefront in responding to conflicts in the world? How do our internal disagreements and differences keep us from being able to have a greater impact on the world?

From the Commentary

> The popular religious philosophy of today is "The Lord helps those who help themselves." It was also popular in Paul's day, and it is just as wrong today as it was then.… The Bible has nothing good to say about flesh, and yet most people today depend entirely on what they themselves can do to please God. Flesh only corrupts God's way on earth (Gen. 6:12). It profits nothing as far as

spiritual life is concerned (John 6:63). It has nothing good in it (Rom. 7:18). No wonder we should put no confidence in the flesh!

—*Be Joyful,* page 99

7. In what ways do you see this philosophy ("The Lord helps those who help themselves") in practice in our world? In the church? Why is this such a compelling philosophy? What steps must be taken to stop putting so much confidence in the flesh?

From the Commentary

Paul was not speaking from an ivory tower; he personally *knew* the futility of trying to attain salvation by means of good works. As a young student, he had sat at the feet of Gamaliel, the great rabbi (Acts 22:3). His career as a Jewish religious leader was a promising one (Gal. 1:13–14), and yet Paul gave it all up—to become a hated member of the "Christian sect" and a preacher of the gospel.

—*Be Joyful,* page 100

8. What attitude does Paul seem to have in Philippians 3:7–11? What sorts of sacrifices do Christians often have to make in order to be true to their faith? Is it easy to have a good attitude about these sacrifices? Why or why not?

9. Reread Philippians 3:7–9. What does it look like to "consider everything a loss" compared to knowing Christ? How is sharing in Jesus' sufferings an example of this?

More to Consider: Read Romans 9:30—10:13. What similarities do you see in this passage to what Paul is saying in Philippians 3:1–11? Why is it so hard to let go of our own "righteousness" and accept the free gift of the righteousness of Christ?

From the Commentary

> When he became a Christian, it was not the *end* for Paul, but the *beginning*. His experience with Christ was so tremendous that it transformed his life. And this experience continued in the years to follow. It was a *personal* experience ("That I may know him") as Paul walked with Christ, prayed, obeyed His will, and sought to glorify His name. When he was living under law, all Paul had was a set of rules. But now he had a Friend, a Master, a constant Companion.
>
> —*Be Joyful,* page 104

10. Read Ephesians 1:15–23 and 3:13–21, then write a description of what resurrection power is. How do you see this resurrection power evidenced in your life and the lives of those around you?

Looking Inward

Take a moment to reflect on all that you've explored thus far in this study of Philippians 3:1–11. Review your notes and answers and think about how each of these things matters in your life today.

Tips for Small Groups: To get the most out of this section, form pairs or trios and have group members take turns answering these questions. Be honest and as open as you can in this discussion, but most of all, be encouraging and supportive of others. Be sensitive to those who are going through particularly difficult times and don't press for people to speak if they're uncomfortable doing so.

11. In what ways are you like the Judaizers who demanded more than simple "faith in Christ" for people to become Christians? (Their requirement was circumcision. Yours might be a way of life, a certain theology, or ritual, etc.) How does this make you feel?

12. How do you put confidence in "the flesh"? Why do you do this? What would your life look like if you put your confidence in Christ instead? Is this easy to do? What obstacles must you overcome to do this well?

13. Describe what "resurrection power" looks like in your life today. In what ways do you share in Christ's sufferings? How can you see joy in this?

Going Forward

14. Think of one or two things that you have learned that you'd like to work on in the coming week. Remember that this is all about quality, not quantity. It's better to work on one specific area of life and do it well than to work on many and do poorly (or to be so overwhelmed that you simply don't try).

Do you need to let go of "requirements" for faith like the Judaizers had? Do you need to learn what it means to "consider everything a loss compared to the surpassing greatness of knowing Christ Jesus"? Perhaps you are feeling a specific prompting to live out some truth you've discovered in the Bible. Write these thoughts below. Be specific. Go back through

Philippians 3:1–11 and put a star next to the verse or phrase that speaks to your heart's greatest need for spiritual growth. Consider memorizing this verse so it can challenge you and move you toward positive change.

Real-Life Application Ideas: Make a list of values you held in high regard before you became a Christian and those you hold in high regard today. What stands out as you compare these lists? Are there old values you still hang onto that you need to let go? Think of ways you can move toward doing this.

Seeking Help

15. Write a prayer below (or simply pray one in silence), inviting God to work on your mind and heart in the areas you noted above. Be honest about your desires and fears.

Notes for Small Groups:

- *Look for ways to put into practice the things you wrote in the Going Forward section in this lesson. Talk with other group members about your ideas and commit to being accountable to one another.*

- *During the coming week, ask the Holy Spirit to continue to reveal truth to you from what you've read and studied.*

- *Before you start the next lesson, read Philippians 3:12–16. For more in-depth lesson preparation, read chapter 9, "Let's Win the Race!" in* Be Joyful.

---

* "Elton John: Religion creates 'hateful lemmings," *MSNBC.com*, November 11, 2006, http://www.msnbc.msn.com/id/15675821/ (accessed September 7, 2007).

The Race
(PHILIPPIANS 3:12–16)

Before you begin ...
- *Pray for the Holy Spirit to reveal truth and wisdom as you go through this lesson.*
- *Read Philippians 3:12–16. This lesson references chapter 9 in Be Joyful. It will be helpful for you to have your Bible and a copy of the commentary available as you work through this lesson.*

Getting Started

From the Commentary

In Philippians 3, Paul gave us his spiritual biography: his past (Phil. 3:1–11), his present (Phil. 3:12–16), and his future (Phil. 3:17–21). We have already met Paul "the accountant," who discovered new values when he met Jesus Christ. In this section we meet Paul "the athlete" with his spiritual vigor, pressing toward the finish line in the Christian race. In the final section we will see Paul "the alien," having his citizenship in heaven and looking for the coming of Jesus Christ. In each of these experiences, Paul was exercising the *spiritual mind;* he was looking at things on earth from God's point of view. As a result, he was not upset by things behind him, around him, or before him—*things* did not rob him of his joy!

—*Be Joyful,* pages 109–10

1. What aspects of the Christian life feel like a race to you? How would you rewrite Philippians 3:12–14 to reflect the current challenges of your race?

More to Consider: Paul uses a variety of metaphors to describe the Christian life—from military to agriculture to athletics. What other metaphors can you think of that fit the Christian life as you know it?

2. Choose one verse or phrase from Philippians 3:12–16 that stands out to you. This could be something you're intrigued by, something that makes you uncomfortable, something that puzzles you, something that resonates with you, or just something you want to examine further. Write that here. What strikes you about this verse?

Going Deeper

From the Commentary

> It is important to note that Paul was not telling us how
> to be saved. If he were, it would be a picture of salvation
> by works or self-effort, and this would contradict what he
> wrote in the first eleven verses of Philippians 3. In order
> to participate in the Greek games, the athlete had to be a
> citizen. He did not run the race to gain his citizenship. In
> Philippians 3:20, Paul reminded us that "our conversa-
> tion [citizenship] is in heaven." Because we are already
> the children of God through faith in Christ, we have the
> responsibility of running the race and achieving the goals
> God has set for us.
>
> —*Be Joyful,* page 110

3. Look up James 2:14–26. How does Paul's message in Philippians
3:12–16 fit with what James teaches? How do the "deeds" James is writing
about impact our attempt to reach for the "prize" Paul talks about?

From the Commentary

> Many Christians are self-satisfied because they compare their "running" with that of other Christians, usually those who are not making much progress. Had Paul compared himself with others, he would have been tempted to be proud and perhaps to let up a bit. After all, there were not too many believers in Paul's day who had experienced all that he had! But Paul did not compare himself with others; he compared himself with *himself* and with *Jesus Christ*. The dual use of the word *perfect* in Philippians 3:12 and 15 explains his thinking. He has not arrived yet at perfection (Phil. 3:12), but he is "perfect" [mature] (Phil. 3:15), and one mark of this maturity is the knowledge that he is *not* perfect! The mature Christian honestly evaluates himself and strives to do better.
>
> —*Be Joyful,* pages 111–12

4. What are some ways Christians compare themselves to other Christians? How does Paul's approach of "comparing himself with himself and with Jesus Christ" instead of with other Christians impact the way he approaches the Christian life?

More to Consider: Wiersbe writes that self-evaluation can be dangerous because we can err in a couple of ways: making ourselves out to be better than we are or worse than we are. What does each of these mistakes say about the person making the wrong judgment? How can such mistakes impact the person's Christian witness?

From the Commentary

The believer must devote himself to running the Christian race. No athlete succeeds by doing everything; he succeeds by *specializing*. There are those few athletes who seem proficient in many sports, but they are the exception. The winners are those who concentrate, who keep their eyes on the goal and let nothing distract them. They are devoted entirely to their calling.

—*Be Joyful,* page 113

5. What does it mean for a believer to "specialize" in the Christian race? What sorts of distractions are the most challenging to believers?

More to Consider: Read Proverbs 9:10. What does the author mean by the "fear of the Lord"? Skim through the rest of Proverbs and underline the descriptions of wisdom that capture your attention.

From Today's World

The sports pages are peppered with stories about athletes who have been caught taking steroids to speed or enhance the process of building muscle mass. Even though the negative side effects of steroids—which include depression and aggressive behavior—are well documented, student athletes and professionals alike continue to inject themselves with the dangerous drug.

6. Are there parallels in the Christian race to steroids? If so, what sort of shortcuts to the prize do Christians attempt? Are there any negative side effects to these shortcuts? Paul seems to suggest the race is long and tiring. What does this say about these shortcuts?

From the Commentary

"Forgetting those things which are behind" does not suggest an impossible feat of mental and psychological gymnastics by which we try to erase the sins and mistakes of the past. *It simply means that we break the power of the past by living for the future.* We cannot change the past, but we can change the *meaning* of the past.

—*Be Joyful,* page 114

7. In what ways does remembering the past make it more difficult to press on toward the prize? What are some examples of "changing the meaning" of the past?

More to Consider: Read 1 Timothy 1:12–17 to discover some of the weights that could have held Paul back. How did these possible obstacles become inspirations?

From the Commentary

"I press." This same verb is translated "I follow after" in Philippians 3:12, and it carries the idea of intense endeavor. The Greeks used it to describe a hunter eagerly pursuing his prey. A man does not become a winning athlete by listening to lectures, watching movies, reading books, or cheering at the games. He becomes a winning athlete by getting into the game and determining to win!

—*Be Joyful,* page 115

8. What does Paul's admonition to "press on" suggest about the role of the church? What does it suggest about how believers ought to approach the daily living-out of their faith? What does it mean to "get into the game" in our Christian lives?

From the Commentary

It is not enough to run hard and win the race; the runner must also obey the rules. In the Greek games, the judges were very strict about this. Any infringement of the rules disqualified the athlete. He did not lose his citizenship (though he disgraced it), but he did lose his privilege to participate and win a prize. In Philippians 3:15–16, Paul emphasized the importance of the Christian remembering the spiritual rules laid down in the Word.

—*Be Joyful,* page 116

9. What are these "spiritual rules" Wiersbe is referring to in Paul's writing? According to Paul, how do we train for the race? What could be the consequences of not running the race properly in our Christian lives?

From the Commentary

> Bible history is filled with people who began the race with great success but failed at the end because they disregarded God's rules. They did not lose their salvation, but they did lose their rewards (1 Cor. 3:15). It happened to Lot (Gen. 19), Samson (Judg. 16), Saul (1 Sam. 28; 31), and Ananias and Sapphira (Acts 5). And it can happen to us.
>
> —*Be Joyful,* page 117

10. Read about one or more of the characters Wiersbe lists above. What "spiritual rules" did they disregard? How might their stories have been different if they'd followed those spiritual rules? How is following spiritual rules different from being tied to the Law? Where does grace fit in this puzzle?

Looking Inward

Take a moment to reflect on all that you've explored thus far in this study of Philippians 3:12–16. Review your notes and answers and think about how each of these things matters in your life today.

> *Tips for Small Groups: To get the most out of this section, form pairs or trios and have group members take turns answering these questions. Be honest and as open as you can in this discussion, but most of all, be encouraging and supportive of others. Be sensitive to those who are going through particularly difficult times and don't press for people to speak if they're uncomfortable doing so.*

11. Have you ever had moments when you felt like you'd "arrived" in your Christian race? What happened to show you that you still had more race to run? What did you learn from that experience?

12. How good are you at forgetting what is behind? What specific things in your past make it difficult for you to press forward? Are there ways you can reframe those memories so they free you to grow? Describe what you think that might take.

13. What is the goal God has called you to? What are some practical ways to keep your eyes focused on Jesus as you pursue that goal?

Going Forward

14. Think of one or two things that you have learned that you'd like to work on in the coming week. Remember that this is all about quality, not quantity. It's better to work on one specific area of life and do it well than to work on many and do poorly (or to be so overwhelmed that you simply don't try).

Do you need to work on forgetting what is behind? Do you need to make intentional decisions to train for your race? How would you do that? Perhaps you are feeling a specific prompting to live out some truth you've discovered in the Bible. Write these thoughts below. Be specific. Go back through Philippians 3:12–16 and put a star next to the phrase or verse that is most encouraging to you. Consider memorizing this verse so that it can bring you encouragement at all times.

Real-Life Application Ideas: Learn what it takes to train for a marathon or other sporting activity. Talk with athletes or research their training regimen online. You might even want to consider training for your own race or sporting activity. As you learn about the training or do your own training, consider how this is like the way Paul encourages you to train your faith. Then apply the same skills and determination to your spiritual growth.

Seeking Help

15. Write a prayer below (or simply pray one in silence), inviting God to work on your mind and heart in the areas you noted above. Be honest about your desires and fears.

Notes for Small Groups:

- *Look for ways to put into practice the things you wrote in the Going Forward section in this lesson. Talk with other group members about your ideas and commit to being accountable to one another.*
- *During the coming week, ask the Holy Spirit to continue to reveal truth to you from what you've read and studied.*
- *Before you start the next lesson, read Philippians 3:17–21. For more in-depth lesson preparation, read chapter 10, "Living in the Future Tense," in* Be Joyful.

The Not Yet
(PHILIPPIANS 3:17–21)

Before you begin ...
- *Pray for the Holy Spirit to reveal truth and wisdom as you go through this lesson.*
- *Read Philippians 3:17–21. This lesson references chapter 10 in* Be Joyful. *It will be helpful for you to have your Bible and a copy of the commentary available as you work through this lesson.*

Getting Started

From the Commentary

How strange in a letter filled with joy to find Paul *weeping*. Perhaps he was weeping over himself and his difficult situation. No, he was a man with a *single mind,* and his circumstances did not discourage him. Was he weeping because of what some of the Roman Christians were doing to him? No, he had the *submissive mind* and would not permit people to rob him of his joy. These tears were not for himself at all; they were shed because of others. Because Paul had the *spiritual mind,* he was heartbroken over the way some professed Christians were living, people who "mind earthly things."

—*Be Joyful,* page 121

1. Have you ever felt like Paul in this passage? What saddens you most when you think of those who are "enemies of the cross"?

2. Choose one verse or phrase from Philippians 3:17–21 that stands out to you. This could be something you're intrigued by, something that makes you uncomfortable, something that puzzles you, something that resonates with you, or just something you want to examine further. Write that here. What strikes you about this verse?

Going Deeper

From the Commentary

To be "spiritually minded" simply means to look at earth from heaven's point of view. "Give your heart to the heavenly things, not to the passing things of earth" (Col. 3:2 PH).... D. L. Moody used to scold Christians for being "so heavenly minded they were no earthly good," and that exhortation still needs to be heeded. Christians have a dual citizenship—on earth and in heaven—and our citizenship in heaven ought to make us better people here on earth. The spiritually minded believer is not attracted by the things of this world. He makes his decisions on the basis of eternal values and not the passing fads of society.

—*Be Joyful,* page 122

3. How do believers live with "dual citizenships"? What causes believers to become too "heavenly minded"? Too "earthly minded"? What are some practical ways to keep that dual citizenship in balance?

From the Commentary

> Those who "mind earthly things" *talk* about earthly
> things. After all, what comes out of the mouth reveals
> what is in the heart (Matt. 12:34–37). The unsaved per-
> son does not understand the things of God's Spirit (1 Cor.
> 2:14–16), so how can he talk about them intelligently?
>
> —*Be Joyful,* page 124

4. The fact that the unsaved person doesn't understand the things of God's
Spirit offers evidence as to why it's often difficult to talk with nonbelievers
about faith. What are some examples of this difficulty in your experience?
What does this tell us about the role of the Holy Spirit in how we
communicate our faith to nonbelievers?

From the Commentary

> But speaking heaven's language not only involves what
> we say, but also the way we say it. The spiritually minded

Christian doesn't go around quoting Bible verses all day! But he is careful to speak in a manner that glorifies God.

—*Be Joyful*, page 124

5. What does the "spiritually minded Christian" sound like to you? Who are some of those Christians in your life? In what ways do they live out the Pauline truth Wiersbe describes above? How is speaking in a manner that glorifies God an example of "living in the future tense"?

More to Consider: Read Ephesians 4:29 and James 3:1–12. What additional insights do these passages add?

From the History Books

When taken to an extreme, Paul's encouragement to live in the future tense—the eager awaiting of a Savior—can lead people to live for heaven with little regard for their earthly lives. One example of this comes from the Millerite movement, a movement started by William Miller, who, after what he believed were careful and accurate calculations, predicted that

Jesus would return in 1843. One of the challenges Miller faced as the date approached was that some of his followers stopped worrying about earthly things: They sold their possessions and began to remove themselves from the daily routine. It became such an issue that leaders had to remind them to "occupy until He comes"—to continue living life in the present while awaiting the future coming.

6. How might believers' lives be different if they lived as if Jesus might return in any given moment? What does it look like to "occupy" until Jesus returns?

From the Commentary

By faith, Paul obeyed the Word of God, knowing that one day he would be rewarded. Men might oppose him and persecute him now, but in that final day of reckoning, he would be the winner.

—*Be Joyful,* page 125

7. What sort of persecution do Christians face today? What are the challenges in the workplace? In friendships? In popular culture? How do believers obey the Word of God in each of these arenas?

8. Reread Philippians 3:18–19. Paul seems to be writing about Christians in this passage, and yet he says their destiny is "destruction." How would you interpret that comment? How do Christians whose god is "their stomach" differ from those who have citizenship in heaven?

From the Commentary

The Judaizers were living in the past tense, trying to get the Philippian believers to go back to Moses and the law, but true Christians live in the future tense, anticipating the return of their Savior (Phil. 3:20–21). As the *accountant* in Philippians 3:1–11, Paul discovered new *values*. As the *athlete* in Philippians 3:12–16, he displayed new *vigor*. Now as the *alien*, he experiences a new *vision:* "We look for the Saviour." It is this anticipation of the coming of Christ that motivates the believer with the spiritual mind.

—*Be Joyful,* pages 126–27

9. How do believers actively anticipate Christ's return? How does your church or small group "look for the Savior" on a regular basis? Many churches focus on this topic only at Christmas. As they recall the first arrival of Christ on earth, they then look forward to His second advent, or second coming. What are some ways to spread this anticipation throughout the entire year?

From the Commentary

The citizen of heaven, living on earth, is never discouraged because he knows that his Lord is one day going to return. He faithfully keeps on doing his job lest his Lord return and find him disobedient (Luke 12:40–48). The spiritually minded believer does not live for the things of this world; he anticipates the blessings of the world to come.

—*Be Joyful,* page 127

10. What is your reaction to Wiersbe's claim that the citizen of heaven is "never discouraged"? Paul references this joy when he states the "eagerness" of a believer's wait for Christ's return. How can this expectation help Christians who are facing difficult circumstances? Is true joy possible when things are tough?

Looking Inward

Take a moment to reflect on all that you've explored thus far in this study of Philippians 3:17–21. Review your notes and answers and think about how each of these things matters in your life today.

> *Tips for Small Groups: To get the most out of this section, form pairs or trios and have group members take turns answering these questions. Be honest and as open as you can in this discussion, but most of all, be encouraging and supportive of others. Be sensitive to those who are*

going through particularly difficult times and don't press for people to speak if they're uncomfortable doing so.

11. In what ways are you living out your "dual citizenship" in heaven and on earth? Are you more heavenly minded or earthly minded? Explain.

12. Consider what your speech says about your faith. Are your words glorifying God? Why or why not? What are some ways you might need to work on heavenly minded speech?

13. What are some of the challenges you're facing today that make it difficult to live in the future tense? How can you discover joy in the midst of those circumstances?

Going Forward

14. Think of one or two things that you have learned that you'd like to work on in the coming week. Remember that this is all about quality, not quantity. It's better to work on one specific area of life and do it well than to work on many and do poorly (or to be so overwhelmed that you simply don't try).

Do you long to learn how to live as a citizen of heaven? Do you need to work on how you say things so they better represent your future-mindedness? Perhaps you are feeling a specific prompting to live out some truth you've discovered in the Bible. Write these thoughts below. Be specific. Go back through Philippians 3:17–21 and put a star next to the phrase or verse that is most encouraging to you. Consider memorizing this verse for future encouragement.

Real-Life Application Ideas: Study the Millerite movement or other examples in Christian history where people believed they could predict the second coming of Christ. As you study these stories, look for both the mistakes made and any positive benefits of this "Christ is coming soon" way of thinking. Apply those positive lessons to your life so you can live in the now and the "not yet" with equal sincerity and intensity.

Seeking Help

15. Write a prayer below (or simply pray one in silence), inviting God to work on your mind and heart in the areas you noted above. Be honest about your desires and fears.

Notes for Small Groups:

- *Look for ways to put into practice the things you wrote in the Going Forward section in this lesson. Talk with other group members about your ideas and commit to being accountable to one another.*

- *During the coming week, ask the Holy Spirit to continue to reveal truth to you from what you've read and studied.*

- *Before you start the next lesson, read Philippians 4:1–23. For more in-depth lesson preparation, read chapters 11 and 12, "You Don't Have to Worry!" and "The Secret of Contentment," in* Be Joyful.

Contentment
(PHILIPPIANS 4:1–23)

Before you begin …
- *Pray for the Holy Spirit to reveal truth and wisdom as you go through this lesson.*
- *Read Philippians 4:1–23. This lesson references chapters 11 and 12 in* Be Joyful. *It will be helpful for you to have your Bible and a copy of the commentary available as you work through this lesson.*

Getting Started

From the Commentary

What is worry? The Greek word translated "careful" (anxious) in Philippians 4:6 means "to be pulled in different directions." Our hopes pull us in one direction; our fears pull us the opposite direction; and we are pulled apart! The Old English root from which we get our word *worry* means "to strangle." If you have ever really worried, you know how it does strangle a person. In fact, worry has definite physical consequences: headaches, neck pains, ulcers, even back pains. Worry affects our thinking, our digestion, and even our coordination.

—*Be Joyful,* page 131

1. What is your first reaction to Wiersbe's explanation of *worry*? In what way is worry an example of wrong thinking? How does worry steal from joy?

2. Choose one verse or phrase from Philippians 4:1–23 that stands out to you. This could be something you're intrigued by, something that makes you uncomfortable, something that puzzles you, something that resonates with you, or just something you want to examine further. Write that here. What strikes you about this verse?

Going Deeper

From the Commentary

Paul did not write, "Pray about it!" He was too wise to do that. He used three different words to describe "right praying": *prayer, supplication,* and *thanksgiving.* Right praying involves all three. The word *prayer* is the general word for making requests known to the Lord. It carries the idea of adoration, devotion, and worship. Whenever we find ourselves worrying, our first action ought to be to get alone with God and worship Him. Adoration is what is needed. We must see the greatness and majesty of God! ... The first step in right praying is *adoration.* The second is *supplication,* an earnest sharing of our needs and problems.... After adoration and supplication comes *appreciation,* giving thanks to God.

—*Be Joyful,* pages 132–33

3. Paul encourages his readers to rejoice always (v. 4), then talks briefly about right praying (v. 6). How can right praying lead to joy? In what ways does prayer bring peace? Contentment?

From the Commentary

> Paul counseled us to take everything to God in prayer. "Don't worry about *anything,* but pray about *everything!*" was his admonition (see Phil. 4:6). We are prone to pray about the "big things" in life and forget to pray about the so-called "little things"—until they grow and become big things! Talking to God about *everything* that concerns us and Him is the first step toward victory over worry.
>
> —*Be Joyful,* page 133

4. What are examples of the big things people tend to pray for? What are some of the little things we forget? Why do we overlook the little things? Is it possible to bring everything to God in prayer as Paul writes? How can we accomplish that?

More to Consider: Read Daniel 6:1–10. How did Daniel pray in this circumstance? How does this match Paul's description of "right praying"? What was the result of his prayer?

5. Reread Philippians 4:8. Circle the descriptive words Paul uses to explain what we should think about. What are examples of each of these? What does it mean to "think on these things"?

From Today's World

According to the A. C. Nielsen Co., the average American will have spent 9 years of his or her life watching TV. By age 65, the average person will have viewed 2 million commercials. By age 18, he or she will have viewed 200,000 violent acts on TV. It is no secret that television has captured the minds (and time) of American culture. As if to underline this fact, there are an average of 2.24 televisions in each household.

6. How much of the television content watched by Americans would you think fits in Paul's definition of what is "true, noble, right, pure, lovely, admirable, excellent, and praiseworthy"? What does this tell you about how well we are doing at thinking on good things? What other distractions cause us to think on detrimental things? Does this mean we are supposed to turn away from all things that aren't good? Why or why not?

From the Commentary

> It is one thing to *learn* a truth, but quite another to *receive*
> it inwardly and make it a part of our inner man (see 1
> Thess. 2:13). Facts in the head are not enough; we must
> also have truths in the heart. In Paul's ministry, he not
> only *taught* the Word but also *lived* it so that his listeners
> could see the truth in his life. Paul's experience ought
> to be our experience. We must learn the Word, receive
> it, hear it, and do it. "Be ye doers of the word, and not
> hearers only" (James 1:22).
>
> —*Be Joyful,* page 136

7. What are some examples of what happens when people learn the
truth but don't live it? Underline some of the truths Paul writes about in
Philippians 4:1–9. How would you go about putting these into practice?

From the Commentary

> The apostle Paul was a thermostat. Instead of having
> spiritual ups and downs as the situation changed, he went
> right on, steadily doing his work and serving Christ. His

personal references at the close of this letter indicate that he was not the victim of circumstances but the victor over circumstances: I can accept all things (Phil. 4:11); "I can do all things" (Phil. 4:13); I have all things (Phil. 4:18). Paul did not have to be pampered to be content; he found his contentment in the spiritual resources abundantly provided by Christ.

—*Be Joyful*, page 141

8. What tempts people to become victims of circumstance? How does popular culture speak to the concept of contentment? How do Paul's words in Philippians 4:10–19 speak to the definition of *contentment*? What challenges does popular culture present that makes it difficult to be content?

From the Commentary

Paul was quick to let his friends know that he was not complaining. His happiness did not depend on circumstances or things; his joy came from something deeper, something apart from either poverty or prosperity.

—*Be Joyful*, page 143

9. As you consider what you've learned of Paul's story in Philippians, why do you think he is able to be content in any circumstance? How do trials and tribulation help train us to be content? Perhaps you've had seasons of being "in need" and seasons of "plenty." In what ways can you feel contentment in each? Is it easier to find contentment in one over the other? Why do you think Paul speaks to both of these in this letter?

From the Commentary

Contentment comes from adequate resources. Our resources are the providence of God, the power of God, and the promises of God. These resources made Paul sufficient for every demand of life, and they can make us sufficient too.

—*Be Joyful,* page 147

10. Describe what each of these "adequate resources" is according to Paul. How do we access these resources? In what ways does contentment bring joy?

Looking Inward

Take a moment to reflect on all that you've explored thus far in this study of Philippians 4:1–23. Review your notes and answers and think about how each of these things matters in your life today.

> *Tips for Small Groups: To get the most out of this section, form pairs or trios and have group members take turns answering these questions. Be honest and as open as you can in this discussion, but most of all, be encouraging and supportive of others. Be sensitive to those who are going through particularly difficult times and don't press for people to speak if they're uncomfortable doing so.*

11. How good are you at not being anxious about things? What sorts of things cause you the most worry? Can you recall a time when you were able to rejoice in a difficult time? What allowed you to be joyful?

12. Take a moment to review all that you pour into your life. How much of what you ingest is "pure, lovely, admirable, excellent, or praiseworthy"? What are things you think on that you probably ought to avoid? What would it take to avoid some of those thoughts?

13. What brings you the most contentment in life? How much do you depend on God for your contentment? What can you learn from Paul's example of contentment to help you become more joyful?

Going Forward

14. Think of one or two things that you have learned that you'd like to work on in the coming week. Remember that this is all about quality, not quantity. It's better to work on one specific area of life and do it well than to work on many and do poorly (or to be so overwhelmed that you simply don't try).

Do you need to learn how to be content? To discover joy in all circumstances? Perhaps you are feeling a specific prompting to live out some truth you've discovered in the Bible. Write these thoughts below. Be specific. Go back through Philippians 4:1–23 and put a star next to the phrase or verse that expresses what you need to work on most. Consider memorizing this verse and putting it into action.

Real-Life Application Ideas: Keep a notepad handy the next time you watch TV. Every time you see or hear an example of the world's definition of contentment ("the more we have, the happier we are") make a check mark. Every time you see an example of Paul's definition, draw a circle. After an hour or so, review your tally. What does this tell you about the message television is promoting? Where can you go to find positive messages that support Paul's definition?

Seeking Help

15. Write a prayer below (or simply pray one in silence), inviting God to work on your mind and heart in the areas you noted above. Be honest about your desires and fears.

Notes for Small Groups:

- *Look for ways to put into practice the things you wrote in the Going Forward section in this lesson. Talk with other group members about your ideas and commit to being accountable to one another.*
- *During the coming week, ask the Holy Spirit to continue to reveal truth to you from what you've read and studied.*

Summary and Review

Notes for Small Groups: This session is a summary and review of this book. Because of that, it is shorter than the previous lessons. If you are using this in a small-group setting, consider combining this lesson with a time of fellowship or a shared meal.

Before you begin …
- *Pray for the Holy Spirit to reveal truth and wisdom as you go through this lesson.*
- *Briefly review the notes you made in the previous sessions. You'll be referring to previous chapters throughout this bonus lesson.*

Looking Back

1. Over the past eight lessons, you've been examining what it means to discover joy in all circumstances. Now that you've spent lots of time with

Paul's letter to the Philippians, how would you define this joy Paul writes about? Has your definition changed at all? Why or why not?

2. What is the most significant personal discovery you've made from this study of Philippians?

3. What surprised you most about the book of Philippians? What, if anything, troubled you?

Progress Report

4. Take a few moments to review the Going Forward sections in the previous lessons. How would you rate your progress for each of the things you chose to work on? What adjustments, if any, do you need to make to continue on the path to discovering how to be joyful?

5. In what ways have you grown closer to Christ during this study? Take a moment to celebrate those things. Then think of areas where you feel you still need to grow and note those here. Make plans to revisit this study in a few weeks to review your growing faith.

Things to Pray About

6. It's not easy to imagine being joyful when facing trials. You may even feel it's impossible at times. Take a few minutes to pray for a greater

understanding of God's truth in this letter and for God to reveal to you just what He wants you to discover among all the wisdom Paul presents.

7. You will probably find that some days are better than others when it comes to discovering joy. Take a few minutes to ask God to help cement the learning in your heart so joy becomes second nature.

8. Whether you've been studying this in a small group or on your own, there are many other Christians working through the very same issues you discovered when exploring Philippians. Take time to pray for each of them, that God would reveal truth, that the Holy Spirit would guide them, and that each person might grow in spiritual maturity according to God's will.

A Blessing of Encouragement

Studying the Bible is one of the best ways to learn how to be more like Christ. Thanks for taking this step. In closing, let this blessing precede you and follow you into the next week while you continue to marinate in God's Word:

May God light your path to greater understanding as you review the truths found in the book of Philippians and consider how they can help you grow closer to Christ.

Be Transformed by GOD'S WORD

THE *Transformation* STUDY BIBLE

Don't copy the behavior and customs of this world, but let God transform you into a new person by changing the way you think. Then you will learn to know God's will for you, which is good and pleasing and perfect. —Romans 12:2

NLT

The Transformation Study Bible
General Editor: Warren W. Wiersbe

Now you can get more from your study of Scripture. Available for the first time, the trusted commentary of Pastor Warren Wiersbe's "BE" commentary series has been excerpted and included alongside the easy-to-read *New Living Translation* text. Accessible and insightful, it's an essential resource for growing motivated disciples.

Available at a Christian bookstore near you or at DavidCCook.com.

1.800.323.7543 • www.DavidCCook.com

David C Cook
transforming lives together